Ramón is the biggest reason
I have gotten where I am.
He is the great one in this family.
I am still Ramón's little brother.

— PEDRO MARTÍNEZ, 1998

FOR WILLIAM, CAITLIN, AND LIAM

Candlewick Press, 99 Dover Street, Somerville, Massachusetts 02144. visit us at www.candlewick.com.
Printed in Shenzhen, Guangdong, China. 14 15 16 17 18 19 CCP 10 9 8 7 6 5 4 3 2 1

GROWING UP PEDRO

MATT TAVARES

CANDLEWICK PRESS

THE DOMINICAN REPUBLIC, 1981

One sunny day in the
village of Manoguayabo,
Pedro Martínez sits in the shade
and watches the older boys play.
He wants to play, too.
But his big brother, Ramón, says he is too little.
The boys are using a hard ball,
and Ramón says it's too dangerous.
Pedro is mad, but he knows
Ramón is just looking out for him.
Ramón is always looking out for Pedro.

Despite his anger, Pedro watches Ramón pitch.
He is the greatest pitcher Pedro has ever seen.

Pedro has three brothers and two sisters.
Ramón, the oldest, is the baseball star of the family.

Pedro wishes he were tall, like Ramón.
He wishes he could throw hard, like Ramón.
He spends hours out behind
the little shack where they live,
throwing rocks at the mango trees.
He tries to hit only the ripe ones,
just like Ramón taught him.

Pedro loves playing baseball.
He dreams that someday
he and his brothers will play
together in the major leagues.
At night, they lie awake,
two to a mattress, and talk about what
they will do when they are millionaires.

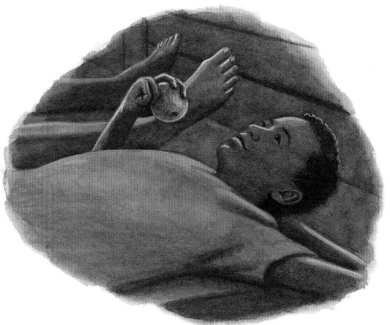

By the time Ramón is fifteen,
he is pitching against grown men
in games around Santo Domingo.
Sometimes Pedro walks for miles
just to watch him pitch.

At sixteen, Ramón is the youngest player
on the Dominican national team.
The Los Angeles Dodgers offer him a contract.
They pay him five thousand dollars —
not much by big-league standards,
but more money than the Martínez
family has ever seen.

Ramón uses some of the money
to buy his little brother Pedro
his first real baseball glove.

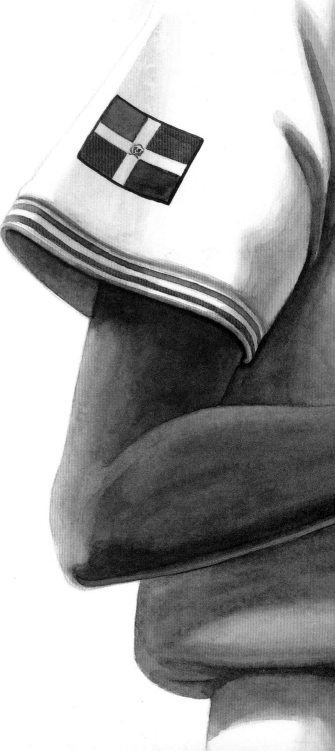

In 1984, when Pedro is twelve,
Ramón starts training at Campo Las Palmas,
the Dodgers' Dominican baseball academy,
a two-hour bus ride from Manoguayabo.
Every chance he gets, Pedro tags along.

Sometimes he even gets to play catch
with Ramón on the field before practice.
For Pedro, it is like a dream.
He can't believe he is on a real baseball field
with real professional ballplayers.
He is so proud of his big brother.

One day, a coach for the Dodgers
watches Pedro pitching to Ramón.
The coach tells Pedro that if he works hard,
maybe someday the Dodgers will sign him, too.

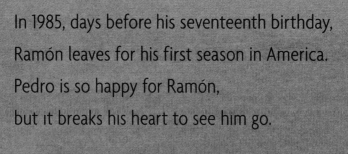

In 1985, days before his seventeenth birthday,
Ramón leaves for his first season in America.
Pedro is so happy for Ramón,
but it breaks his heart to see him go.

Now that Ramón is gone,
Pedro is more determined than ever
to make it to the major leagues.
Every day, he practices and practices.

For Ramón, adjusting to life in America is not easy.
When his team stops to eat at a restaurant,
he doesn't know what to order
because all the menus are in English.
He can't talk to anyone.

Ramón tells Pedro all about it.
He wants to make sure that when it's Pedro's turn,
his little brother is ready.

Pedro keeps practicing,
and he starts studying English every day.
In 1988, when he is sixteen,
Pedro is back at Campo Las Palmas.
He is ready to try out for the Dodgers.
Dozens of other boys are trying out, too.
Most of them are much bigger
and stronger than Pedro.

He works hard and does his best.
But the Dodger scouts aren't sure.
He is still so much smaller than Ramón.
They worry that he just isn't big enough
to make it in professional baseball.

Finally, after a thirty-day tryout,
the Dodgers decide to give Pedro a chance.
They pay him six thousand, five hundred dollars.
He gives all the money to Ramón.

In 1990, the Dodgers assign Pedro to their
minor-league team in Great Falls, Montana.
Pedro says good-bye to his family
and leaves for America.